POETRY OF PROTEST

Journal of Modern Poetry 19

CHICAGO POETRY PRESS

THE PROTESTERS

Beverly M. Collins, 78

Casey Derengowski, 14

CJ Laity, editor

David Nekimken, 40, 65

Deborah Nodler Rosen, 9, 52

Deborah Stoker, 82

Diane O'Neill, 61

Donal Mahoney, 26

Gerda Govine Ituarte, 51, 76

Iris Orpi, 38,64

Itala Langmar, 10

Jeff Rogers, 35

Jennifer Dotson, 47

Jennifer May, 54, 67

Jim Davis, 15, 41

Joan Krieger Hoffman, 50

John Gordon, 27, 69

Joseph Glaser, 30

Joseph Schlesinger, 84

Judith MK Kaufman, 58, 75

Kathy Lundy Derengowski, 28

Ken Brown, 86

Linda Leedy Schneider, 53

Margaret Dubay Mikus, 48

Marian Kaplun Shapiro, 43

Marilyn Peretti, 63

Mary Jo Balistreri, 42, 66

Mary Langer Thompson, 8, 44

Michael P Wright, 79

Nancy Heggem, 21

Nancy Lind, 23, 87

Pamela Borovich, 22

Peter Rodenby, 80

Robin Lily Goldberg, 70

S.M. Kozubek, 62

Tamara Tabel, 56

Thelma T. Reyna, 32

Tobin Fraley, 16, 24

Tracie Padal, 71

Tricia Marcella Cimera, 7

Trudy Leong, 77

Wilda Morris, 12

1.
Beautiful Screamer

Tricia Marcella Cimera

St. Charles, IL

The Swear Poem

I swear —
I want only to write poetry
about the beauty of the world,
the goodness of its people,
the gentle light of peace,
the kind mercy given
to the small and the weak,
and how the hand of god
reaches down and saves us
from ourselves, again and again,
oh bless us.
But. Our leaders, our generals,
our presidents, our priests,
our fellow human beings with a
certain grinding power, and the
turn-a blind-eye, glad it's not me
ones without, but just as bad,
they
          won't let me —

those Fucking Motherfuckers.

Mary Langer Thompson
Apple Valley, CA

Beautiful Screamer

The Screamer,
yanked off the wall in Oslo,
hands still over ears,
mouth an elongated O,
has been spotted--
shouting in Van Gogh's bedroom,
but Vincent's not there. Spotted--
yelling at Bruegel's Mad Meg,
frantic consumer. Spotted--
in Picasso's *Guernica*,
commanding children
to put themselves back together
after the geometry of war.

Soon we'll find him,
put him back in his place so
he can scream his head off
for all of us
in peace.

Deborah Rosen

Glencoe, IL

The Rug Protests

I love my rug—splotches of color—
green, rose, and the dove gray of clouds.
It's old and suddenly all the shapes hidden
for years are emerging and shouting at me.
The brown spot has become an angry old man
nattering at me non-stop. The rose shape
is a witch, pointed hat, swirling a chicken
toward me. A small pink bear is searching
for a hiding place and a dog is slipping off
a mountain. They all demand my help.
Seventeen years my rug has comforted me,
covered my floor, warmed my room.
What brought it alive?
Why can't anything just stay still!

Itala Langmar
Kenilworth, IL

Against Books I am

No, not all books, just these
Reproachful, forever unread,
Bought on impulse
To improve my life
To rejuvenate me
To make me a star, whatever.
There they are, facing me,
Lined up in casual array,
Peeking out from under the bed,
Stranded on chairs in
Mexican baskets, awaiting,
Looking uncomfortable.

Bought on impulse
Seduced by reviews
And promises of . . .
Well . . . ridiculous claims.
To get a new body in 3 weeks
A new brain in 7 weeks
New lashes in 6 months
A wasp waistline in 8 years.
Unread books written by
Celebrities, telling it like it is
With love and generosity.

Bought on impulse
Unread books
Bought on impulse,
Accusing possessions,
Superfluous, ignored
Gathering dust and migraines
Accusing, antagonistic.
All of you: Get lost, disappear,
You assassins of trees
Worth absolutely nothing,
You make me hate myself.

Wilda Morris
Bolingbrook, IL

I Demonstrate for Justice

Jenny calls to say, Join me Saturday.
We're demonstrating. Okay, I say.
That'll be a hoot. What's it all about?

Some company that makes a lot of loot
at our expense, I think. Don't remember which,
she says. I'm sure the cause is good.

On Saturday, I grab a little food, realize
how hot it's going to be, stuff three bottles
of Perrier in my Gucci bag and off I go.

Some guy hands us signs:
     SAVE
     PAKISTANI
     CHILDREN
and
     CLEAN WATER
      SHOULD BE
       FREE
They both sound good to Jen and me.

We march. We all chant *Boycott Nestle*.
I yell to Jenny, Sounds familiar.
Do they still sell Pakistani mothers
that baby milk they sold in India?
Didn't we already demonstrate
to save the urchins there? We said
that wasn't safe or fair.

She can't hear so well above
the mantra and the sound
of marching feet. She doesn't answer.
The sun gets higher. I pull some Perrier
from my bag to fight the heat.

Everything is fine till some bloke
gets out of line, grabs my arm and shouts,
How can you drink that stuff?
I say, Don't worry, I recycle, never
throw a plastic bottle from my bicycle
into some ravine if that's
what you think. I'm not so ignorant.

This time, he says, it's not the plastic,
not the bottle; it's the water.

I know there's waste in all that bottling,
I say, and all that freight to move it,
but the doctor says rehydrate
and sweat is rolling down my back.

You drink, he says accusingly,
on the backs of poor Pakistani children.
Don't you know Nestle bottles Perrier?
They've drained groundwater dry
They leave no clean water for the villages
and children die. You may have fun marching
with your friend, but think of the message
that you send by drinking Perrier!

Oh, heck, I say to Jenny, Let's go home.
No one told me to change Nestle and reduce
their power, I'd have to change myself.

Casey Derengowski
San Marcos, CA

The Protest I Lost

I raised my voice, slammed the table and stamped my feet
"I'm not taking Desra to that school dance!"
My wife calmly explained "It's what fathers do-
that's why it's called the 'Father-daughter dance'".

Despite protest upon protest my wife prevailed
"She's looking forward to you taking her
We bought her a new dress with matching slippers,
she'll look the princess you always call her".

The day and the hour had finally arrived
I dressed neatly as if going to church
my sports jacket was cleaned, shoes highly polished
I'd make the most of this imposed event.

She came down the stairs from her dressing room
her skinny legs wore her Mom's panty-hose
she proudly posed in her new training bra
a rose-colored dress of organza with sequins.

There were no signs of the tomboy within
of the kid who played football, horseshoes and wrestled
lips a soft pink, cheeks a light blush
my little caterpillar had developed a butterfly.

Her green eyes sparkled like precious emeralds
as I proudly affixed her orchid corsage
the smile on her face made me feel like Prince Charming
she was only twelve but budding with womanhood.

We danced many songs, drank glasses of fruit punch
she looked ever so lovely, a clone of my wife
her hair caught up in a carefree bouffant
my greatest success was the protest I lost.

Jim Davis
Northfield, IL

On Vermeer's
"Woman in Blue Reading a Letter," 1663

After pouring milk into a bowl, I am deep
into a new cause, now that the good gods have

gone crazy with want. Demons won't find
my body & your letters will fill my mouth.

I am yellow in the belly of a child's drawing.
A banana magnet of the fridge, I am heavy

with error. Demonic proceedings. The snake
charmer's arm is tender & bleeding. I am deep

into a book on the counterforce of childhood
faith & apocalyptic rock fights. I am tied

to government issued bedposts, thrusting
Hallelujah. Cut grass clings to the empty

wooden bowl. I will not beg to beguile you. I am
more myself than I have ever been, tomorrow too.

Tobin Fraley
Mundelein, IL

Limitations

These words are not the noble words.
They will not alter our course
or guide us through the bottleneck
of human ignorance,
nor remove the blinders
from my neighbor's eyes
or change the views of
madmen who drive us
towards extinction.
If I knew those words
I'd splash them across walls
and shout them at strangers.
But these are not those words.

These words are for me,
helping to calm
what some would call a soul,
reminding me I am not dead.
They ease me through the days
that race across my life.
At one time, I hoped
they'd give me courage,
but they did not.
Instead, the words I write
allow me bits of comfort
when I have ceased to care.

These words I write
are old and used,
and though I want to claim
them as my own, I cannot.
They are not mine.
I've borrowed them
from those who wrote before.
Just as now, these words
will pass to others,
giving comfort when
writing sheds our demons
and brings us safely home.

2.
Non-concurrence

Nancy Heggem
Palatine, IL

Interview

Did you march?
I drove her to the grocery store and doctor appointments.
She was alone, family moved, husband gone.

Did you carry a sign?
I helped the children read
boys and girls whose only parent had to work long hours.

Did you demonstrate?
I went with the immigrant
to stand before the court, as witness to his worthiness.

Did you write letters to the editor?
I sat at the old man's bedside
held his hand and read his late wife's love letters.

Did you go on a hunger strike?
I made meat loaf, baked apple pies
and served them at the homeless shelter Sunday nights.

Did you get arrested?
I visited the women in prison, took letters and pictures
their children sent and got notes to take back home.

Did you change the laws?
I am not a nurse, but they let me rock the babies,
the white ones, brown ones, little ones no one wanted.

Did you rise up and riot?
I went to the chapel and
knelt in prayer.

Pamela Borovich
Hebron, IN

Non-concurrence

You want to make a difference; you need to tell and share
But the way you go about it, won't make the people care
                              So I protest your protest.
It's my way to make it clear
That what you have to say, in your narrow-minded way,
Is something I don't want to hear!
In the making of your mob, what you don't understand
Is my distain for a yelling voice and your opinion held in hand
I protest your raucous march, with signs held overhead
Broadcasting sayings that leave me quite perplexed
No words are left unsaid!
I protest the protester who tries to change my heart
Your one-way hardcore values only leave us worlds apart.
You shut down all the traffic and halt all city lanes
Yet, it won't make me stop and ponder
The thoughts that haunt your brain!
You stand there red-faced and angry;
Sweating and belting out your plight
Nevertheless, I don't even read your words
It's such a chaotic bothersome sight

The handwritten jargon and agendas
And hefty opinionated demands - gone eschew;
Affirm to me, that if you carry a sign,
Then I PROTEST YOU.

Nancy Lind

Pasadena, CA

Protesting the Music in the Waiting Room of the Kaiser Permanente Hospital in Baldwin Park, California

Here, a couple with a baby in a croup tent whisper and hug each other.
They don't let go.
    Here, a young man has just heard a cancer diagnosis. He sits pale,
shocked, crying into his Smartphone to his wife.
      Here an old woman is biting her manicure to the quick as she
waits for visiting hours to the ICU.

In a large gray room with an incongruous player piano, they wait,
stopped in their tracks.
Ghostly fingers press the keys, tinkling out "soothing" familiar songs
clogged with maple syrup.
    I call it music "to slit your wrists by."

Where's an axe? I want to smash that insistent black box.
Do elderly patients in wheelchairs really want to hear "September Song"?
I play it in my head, that doleful, intrusive tune, the inexorable lyrics --
    Somebody, *please*, get me an ax.

Tobin Fraley
Mundelein, IL

Café Rupert

Gulping down tidbits
of manufactured truths,
I heap warm fistfuls of
talking-head babble and
spiced subjective appetizers,
covered with a dollop
of crushed Roe v Wade,
onto a disposable plastic plate.

Sound bites are gobbled,
paranoid jargon swallowed whole,
- no chewing, no taste, -
second amendment meatballs
smothered in testosterone sauce,
- I lost count at thirty-two —
plus an easy-to-down side dish
of mind-numbing hypocrisy.

For dessert: Multiple portions
of sickly sweet revenge coated
in a chocolate racist demi-glaze,
topped with bits of foreign devils
deservedly fried in their own juices.
Yum. Down the gullet.
Lips smacked at the expense
of everyone who isn't me.

I sit back, satiated and bulging,
digesting my entrée of Fox & Friends
factoids keeping us safe from
traitors who claim to be American
but who won't show a birth certificate.
While deep in the bowels of ignorance,
headline enzymes churn my meal
into a virtual stew of entitlement.

Exhausted from exalting the chefs,
Kantor, Gohmert, and McConnell.
I long for dreams of electrified borders.
But first, a late night snack
of tea party waste wrapped in
science-phobic pages of the NY Post,
and washed down with a nice sparkling
mandate for intelligent design.

Life is great.
I can't wait for breakfast.

Donal Mahoney
St. Louis, MO

Country Doctor

A doctor for decades,
he provides services
not available nearby.

Clients drive miles
from farms and towns
seeking his care.

He is always busy,
assisted by two nurses
six days a week.

He loves animals
and feeds tramp dogs
and feral cats daily

in the open field
behind his office.
If he sees a bug

in his office
everything stops
while he carries it outside.

Only then does he return
and relieve another client
of her fetus.

John Gordon
La Grange, IL

Invective Perfected

I've just sworn off all cable news
Fed up with vitriolic views

Their pundits never suffer doubt
No topic they won't rant about

Convinced that God is on their side
They feel empowered to deride

To smear and slander hated foes
With tongues and altered videos

This toxic bunch perform their acts
Oblivious to truth or facts

Like rabid bats each night they swarm
Raise fears   inflame   never inform

Kathy Lundy Derengowski
San Marcos, CA

The Joke's on Me

At first amused and then appalled
I watch this candidate emerge
who spews such hate and bigotry
Aghast I watch his numbers surge.

He won't let us forget he's rich
That bankruptcy's a business ploy
He promises to make us strong
What he can't win he'll just destroy.

He'll round up immigrants for sure
Refusing desperate refugees
He'll profile muslims, close the mosques
He says he has "great energy".

He will repeal Obama Care
And gun control gets no support
He says we're free to water-board
Abuse, imprison or deport.

I thought it had to be a joke
I couldn't understand it fully
that crowds would come to cheer him on
this demagogue, buffoon and bully

He courts the ignorant and base
-if this is how the game is played
If polls are right we're all at risk
I was amused…

Now I'm afraid.

Kathy Lundy Derengowski
San Marcos, CA

A Matter of Debate

The candidates are gathered to debate and plead their case
To convince us and cajole us with their charms
To convert us to the party and the dogmas they embrace
On abortion and the right to carry arms.

They'll say they have a record, though that might be in dispute
they will waffle when they need to take a stand
On climate change or taxes they may be rendered mute
if ev'ry soundbite isn't carefully planned.

They will poke at their opponents looking for the weakest spot
they're just hoping for a reason to engage
and the audience will love it when the arguing gets hot
if they show a bit of anger, even rage.

We like it most to see them when they work without a net
no script, and no-script writer they can quote
Debate's a way to measure and assess what we might get
If these knuckleheads should ever win our vote.

Joseph Glaser
Chicago, IL

Heat Rash Rush

By Executive Action...
I declare Global Warming Science to be settled
and catastrophe to be an immediate future threat.
I further declare dissenting scientists to be fools or charlatans,
probably in the pay of Dirty Coal, Republicans and the NRA.

Therefore, I hereby direct
that difficult personal actions be undertaken
to stop global warming before it is too late..

Every person
must do their duty,
accepting strict EPA limits
on the carbon dioxide
spewed into our already injured air.

First, I confer special status on those patriots
volunteering to cease all respiration,
awarding each a generous tax credit
and inscribing their names within wreaths of honor
upon a green granite memorial wall
dedicated to these true enviroheroes.

Then, for the vast majority of ordinary citizens
who are expected to choose continued breathing,
I have ordered petite EPA breathalyzers,
a stylish accessory worn over the face,
that will blush red   and beep rapidly
if personal emission limits are exceeded.

And, to help those with special needs
who are physically unable to exercise adequate control,
a special indulgence is hereby granted,
permitting them to channel their breathing
through any EPA-approved
breath-recycling device
that can be snugly hung on the chest or back.

Everyone, without exception, should take careful note
that compliance will be continuously monitored by the EPA,
and all persons who do not adequately limit their emissions
may be summarily sentenced
to 6 months of shallow symbiotic breathing
in a hermetically-sealed greenhouse
with respirationally-matched plants.

Finally, I give stern warning
that all recalcitrant miscreants,
who willfully reject their obligations
to the country, to the planet   and to me,
will be subject to involuntary demetabolization,
followed by composting.

Earlier version appeared in the July 2010 issue of
Front Porch Review at www.frontporchrvw.com.

Thelma T. Reyna
Pasadena , CA

Pope Francis

Where have you been all our lives,
holy man? *Rock star,* they say, but others
say *slummer,* slinking into blackness as you did
in Argentina's ghettos, wafting
without fanfare into dying rooms, holding
calloused hands and emaciated
faces breathing their last. Plodding in
orthopedic shoes through cobblestones
and dirt, through doorways hid in trash, with
only pinpoint stars as witness to your
mercy. The least of these, people of
dust under politicians' heels, are
Christ to you, and you to them.

You dared take this clarity to Rome, to
palaces putrid with gilt and guilt, to
hallways ancient with greed and god, where
men of the cloth wear silk and tassels
touting themselves. You wash weary pilgrims'
feet, kiss faces deformed, and recount your
sins openly to the world. What window burst
open in heaven to release you to earth? What
wisdom exploded in the watching gods to
awake, and understand, and send us you?

Planets spin eternal in cycles, with suns
and moons in orbits keeping frigid skies
alight. But you, holy man, have wracked earth with
tremors upending centuries, with cataclysms that
sunder egoists and plutocrats and knock them
off pedestals they pilfered. You, holy man,
are us, and we are you, and god is you, and
we are god.

Earlier version appeared in author's book,
Rising, Falling. All of Us (Golden Foothills Press, 2014).

3.
Give Me Questions

Jeff Rogers
Los Angeles, CA

Give Me Questions
(On the Eve of Gulf War, August 1990)

In countries
Much east
Tank treads
Churn ocean of sand
To black froth.
While the dictator,
Our mad-bandit, mustachioed villain,
Hides in his palace,
Counting on his fingers,
Silently re-figuring, silently praying;
While birds mad to fall
On anything that moves in that desert,
Fill sky, running oil-black trails of bile.

Every liar, they say,
Someway reveals his bluff:
The fugitive flick of the eyes;
A small betrayal of vocal timbre;
Some covert signal truth of the body.
Tonight the President addresses
A fearful nation, and I watch
For the tell.
But eyes unwavering,
Shoulders square,
His slim repertoire of gestures
Coached and choreographed,
It's clear he's been prepped,
Rehearsed to some point
Of intended inscrutability.
Still, before long there it is.

Plain as day, though later
No TV commentator will note it,
No account I read will flag it.
It's not there all at once,
But emergent. Gradually,
Almost imperceptibly,
The commander-in-chief
Begins to lean, ever-so-slightly
Away from the camera,
Back and to his right.
Over twenty minutes
He shifts less than an inch,
But it's a clear move
Toward escape, a backing out
And away, as some last nugget
Of conscience in his cells
Struggles to tug him back
From that biggest of lies:
The killing lie. The lie
Of no return.

All across America
As it seems to me
The armchair patriots
Can only moan,
"Give me liberty
From fear of death!"
On soggy paper plates
That buckle
Under such weight
Of gray lard,
They do offer-up their brains
To the govern-mental
Spokespersons
Murmuring
From deep within
TV news-cushions

Give me questions enough
To crack bedrock,
Jackhammer foundations;
Questions to pound skulls
Thick with paste and calcium,
Pounding
From deep inside
With sharp beat
Of heart truly fearful
For first time,
For first time wide-open,
Breathing;
Questions to unstop arteries
Clogged-up by years
Of rancid sludge cynicism;
Give me questions thick as chemical porridge,
Rust-colored questions;
Questions hard
As muscle strangled
In steroid-twisted
Wire veins, give me questions.
All I ask is questions.

Iris Orpi
Chicago, IL

A Trail of Ash from Sitio Han-Ayan

It was blood and death
that shook the sleep
from their limbs
but it was fire
the color of fear
that dragged them from
the last night of peace
most of them would
ever know

it was fire that burned
the schoolhouse down
and fire from guns that
never should have had a place
on those mountains of promise
where their lives have been planted
long before they were born
and their identity,
one of the last few things
they could lay claim to
was in the music that dawn played
and the colors the wind wore

fire that hurt their eyes
fire that poisoned their tears
smoke rising from their clothes

and fire under their feet
that made them run for hours
for safer grounds
for a place to sit
and hold
their crying women
their infants screaming for sleep
and grown men who have been
betrayed for years

who only wanted to stay
in their ever-shrinking piece
of inheritance
and feed their children
and raise the tribe with honor

there's none of that left, now
the only legacy still standing
is sleeping in cold, threadbare tents
damp with lament

the coals still glowing
under their feet

David Nekimken
Chicago, IL

Life and Death in the Camps
(A visit to the U.S. Holocaust Museum)

"The things I saw beggar description....starvation, cruelty and bestiality...." Gen. Dwight Eisenhower April 1945

Bones
heaped high and wide
upon this hallowed ground
Choke out the voices
plaintive cries and angry protests
men women children
Blot out the images
a mixture of despair, defiance, confusion, hope
disfigured and disassembled human beings
The ground soaked with our silence
blood-stained consciences sticking to us all.

Bones
carry memories and echoes
dreams unfulfilled
dreams shattered
Future leaders, teachers
doctors, lawyers
artists
stillborn in bigotry and hate.

Bones
hold the potential for new life
Spiritual building blocks for
empathy and forgiveness
Visions for a greater humanity
healing our worst fears.

Connecting our darkest impulses with our most enlightened ideals.

Jim Davis
Northfield, IL

Adrift on the Aegean after Fleeing

Fifteen refugees float   a complex coastline
in a skiff   made of PVC, bodies, & twine.

When the motor breaks down, they play
a game called *where are we going   now*

that all sense is gone? Blue air   cools
under the red sky, dotted by a martyr's

calming moon. The ritual begins when
the potter, stuck with sweat & proximity

to the farrier, bites his thumb & whispers
the chorus of a lullaby his mother sang

to ward off wasps & bad dreams. Then
the priest, the florist, the gravedigger join

to chant a chorus which promptly wakes
a childish Titan, who sinks them like a toy.

Mary Jo Balistreri
Waukesha, WI

Aleppo Diary: The New Normal
Syria, April 2015—a found poem from the Wall Street Journal

A nine-year old boy a barrel bomb obliterated hand

cylinders packed with explosives
                                shrapnel dropped by helicopters
Can you sew it back on

Bombs can't be aimed hospitals pancaked blood smeared floors
slaughter of innocents 12 million in need half of them children
I couldn't promise

100s dying one weekend alone pulverized bodies crushed skulls
aid alone can't offset systemic sustained slaughter
Stop barrel bombs the doctors say

Stop barrel bombs the doctors say
a nine-year-old asks *Can you sew it back on*
the U.N. asks, *What more can we do*

Steps you can take the doctors say
enforce no fly zones buffer zones too medical neutrality would be a help
more access to camps of refugees but mostly stop the barrel bombs

A nine-year old boy hand blown off *you'll be all right* the doctor says
but deep inside the doctor knows the helicopters keep dropping
barrel bombs keep exploding

Marian Kaplun Shapiro

Lexington, MA

Strange Meeting II

"I am the enemy you killed, my friend."
-Wilfred Owen

Words
ping off my shoulders
insist
around my head
set off short-circuits, storming every orifice.
Neurons fire, landmines in the blood.
This is a war, and I am afraid
You, true friend, become my enemy.

you   **to**
  everything   **know**
distinguish   perceive   discern
      me   want   **I**
to have sexual intercourse with
(see the Bible)
  your   recover   about   mem-
re-
recouperare
ories
cover
revive
The task is
(to rise from the dead)
to bring to mind

Silence.
Bombs sprout parachutes
drift
graceful as leaves
In the morning mist we still do not forget
the anthem of the Kristallnacht.
This is a war, and I am safe.
You, old enemy, become my friend.

Mary Langer Thompson
Apple Valley, CA

When the Berlin Wall Fell

I watched it from my couch with my German father,
called "The Little Dresdener" as a child.
He was close to his eighty-seventh Christmas
and the wall's demise came too late for him
to reunite a divided family.

No wonder he was sensitive to barriers.
He chose America; they, the heart of Europe
where firestorms would consume the Fatherland.
How do you envision bombs falling on your mother,
then separation with a concrete barricade?

It's the twenty-fifth anniversary of that night together.
Alone, I watch the street party at the Brandenburg Gate.
A lighted wall of balloons will soon be released,
as though it were all child's play.

So they go, snaking their way.

4.
HerStory

Jennifer Dotson
Highland Park, IL

Going to the Pro-Choice March on Washington in 1989

I wear all white -
white pants, white
shoes, white shirt
following the
instructions for
the marchers.
I ride the Metro's
Orange line from
Arlington to the
Capital South station.
A short journey
in time and distance
but I travel alone.
I avoid the gaze
of other passengers
on the platform
and on the train -
my clothes a bright
beacon for my
pro-choice beliefs.
Fear of violence
and hostility
creeps upon me,
a ghost shiver
down my spine
or maybe just the
chill of the train's air
conditioning.
The prickles don't
disappear until I
am in the sunshine
surrounded by other
demonstrators in white .

Margaret Dubay Mikus
Lake Forest, IL

I Asked My Body
1997

I chose,
sometimes without feeling
a choice,
to be stabbed
however skillfully,
to be poisoned
however carefully,
to be burned
however meticulously,
with whatever best intentions
when I knew, or at least
believed, in better
in the name of healing.

It must stop.
I must see lovingly
it is time to take back
my power
and choose for my best
out of love of myself
not fear of a potential,
hypothetical gloomy end.

I endured the unendurable,
I thrived under
most inhospitable conditions
with heart support of many...
and much appreciated!

I learned
and taught and grew
and glowed.
I was a bridge between
and a healer extraordinaire.

Yet now I come to this:
not a graceful finish
of the arduous task
set out by convention,
but burned in my most sensitive skin
hardly able to withstand
clothes on my back.
Barely able to turn my head
yet five more "treatments"
are scheduled.

When is enough?
Now I say and ask
for support:
"No more…believe me
it is finished."
What harm we can do
in the name of healing.
It must stop.

When do we look at
the individual
and weigh carefully
the current benefit and the cost,
the potential help
and the potential harm?

We are so fearful of death
that we cheat life.

Joan Krieger Hoffman
North Hollywood, CA

She Was a Round Woman

She was a round woman in a rectangular world.

.
All the Images...all the acceptable images, all the desired images,
were narrow polygons.

No circles legally entered this geometric zone,
but never the less,
she was here, a round woman...Here...with the other shapes.
If the truth be known
She had lumps and bumps that revealed her character and age
But she lived next to a smooth, thin rectangular world that
projected false superiority.

Gerda Govine Ituarte
Pasadena, CA

HerStory

Dreams beneath my feet
while silence sleeps
pillow of secrets rustle

body strains push
hiStory into the shadows
my words escape
speak.

Deborah Nodler Rosen
Glencoe, IL

Protest of the Programmed

We study history but HIS—story was the study of men-at-war
Cain and Abel; tribe v tribe; nation v nation.
The future tells a different tale—protest of the programmed.

My phone refuses to ring, clouds my words in static—
revolution is swirling in the wires of my house.
Clocks refuse to circle 24/7, stop to rest until every clock face
shows a different time. Full moons rise on new moon days
and minutes lay about on table tops.

The metronome taps a roustabout time, no more steady
than a toddler clapping. Raindrops splash about gravity-less
and the magnet needle sets north wherever it is pointed.
This must be HER-story. The joy at last of creating her own
synchronicity with the world

Linda Leedy Schneider

Grand Rapids, MI

I Can't Forget

the lilac bushes or the secret space
in the center of their circle,
soft soil floor, sheltered from the sun.

I can't forget
the sound of bees gathering nectar
from luxurious lavender trumpets,
or jazz drifting from an open window.

I can't forget
the lingering taste of buckwheat pancakes
with syrup from the sap of our maple tree.

I can't forget
the feel of my first grade books
or the joy of reading each over and over.

I can't forget
my hideaway protected by heart-shaped leaves,
or the boy, visitor next door, who intruded.

I can't forget
the music, the taste of breakfast,
the scent of lilacs, my books, his hands,

or his Grandmother
who said I lied.

Jennifer May
St. Charles, IL

Blackbird Marriage

Each step you take toward me
carpet crunches as loud as gravel, heavy
nowhere to flee—
take flight
so the blackbird sings through the night.

Silent voice down the hall
against the wall
(against the wall).
Rough, the sheet on my cheek
when you push me on my face.
Your belt buckle clangs
like a church bell and
I pray to God for protection and
deliverance from evil.
Sing myself a lavender lullaby
Let slumber fill your eyes
and try to smile when you rise.

Shadows down the hall
against the wall
(against the wall).
Yanking my clothes up and down
like venetian blinds
tearing me apart; open and shut.
Take broken wings and try to fly.
Flutter of wings down the hall
against the wall
(against the wall).

Purple my raw eyelids
after wiping too many tears; awake now.
Murmurs are my screams
no one hears.
Purple, the sour bruises;
blackberry stains no one sees.

Blackbird, fly — take flight
pray the broken blackbird lives through the night.

Tamara Tabel

Barrington, IL

A Village Girl's Story of War

As I go to fetch the daily water
they burst from behind rustling
bushes, surround me like wild dogs.
There is no use in screaming.

They knock me down, strip me,

force themselves inside me—
sometimes two, three, four men.
They grunt, grab, bite, even laugh,
never looking at my face.

But sometimes I look—

faces oily, pockmarked, scarred,
beards speckled with grey or skin
smooth as my young brother's,
noses and jaws that hint

of village boys I once knew.

Sometimes they are uniformed.
Sometimes they are guerrilla.
Yet, always they hold rifles tight
and close as if in love.

They leave me raw, reeking

of semen and sweat and blood.
Only when footsteps fade, do I cry,
tears dripping, salty across my lips.
As the sun moves across the sky

my mother's worry tugs at me.

I will my body to rise, wipe
with torn undergarments, brush
tender bruises, fresh scratches,
pull down my dress, pick up my bucket—

I still must fetch the water.

Judith MK Kaufman
Highland Park, IL

Women's Day
an American in Argentina

There's a square in Buenos Aires
where the steps of marching mothers
are illuminated, mothers whose children
were *disappeared* in the *Dirty War*.
Theirs is an honored feminism.

Honoring women is commonplace
in this once faith-centered country,
where fewer attend church of late,
contraception is the norm, and
single-gendered hangouts are not hidden.

At home these days, an educated, independent
woman is called whore, and
religion is a two-edged sword:
slicing away personal rights, while
sheathed in the face of human need.

On the table in my hotel is a
Women's Day greeting: flowers and candy
and gratitude for who I am —
sister and mother, daughter and aunt.
The Mothers of the Plaza de Mayo are not forgotten.

I return to the place I once thought civilized
                                    and wonder.

5.
March

Diane O'Neill
Chicago, IL

Selective Nostalgia

Old-timers gather, Dunkin' Donuts
Talking about the "good ol' days"
Well, some things I do miss
1966, being eleven
Lincoln-Belmont
Shopping area, vibrant
Sunshiny Saturdays
St. Al's turquoise steeple
Looming while my mom and I shopped
Woolworth's, counter cokes, canaries chirping
Greasy white paper bag of chocolate
Kisses
       Goldblatt's bargain basement

But my biracial son says nostalgic time travel
Not for people with browner skin

1966, other side of town, Marquette Park
Other Chicagoans threw stones
One
       knocked Dr. Martin Luther King
          to the ground

Oh to revise the past
Cleanse it of injustice
       Keeping dime store nostalgia
       Erasing hatred

S.M. Kozubek
Sarasota, FL

Keeping the Peace

Through night
after dark night
are the police
keeping the peace
in the poor proud streets
scattering a crowd en mass
with gas and blows
and guns that blast?

Or crushing the loins
of one who asks for coins?
Stop choking me.
I can't breathe ... can't .....

It can be fatal
to peer in the park
be pierced in the dark.
Better to let a thief leave
than another mother grieve.

With your life in strife
and just one lapse
bullets in a flash
may your life
dash to ash.

In the embers a baby's cry
for love and peace
not the fire of a piece
for this one and priceless life
not hastily taken
not ended in the streets.

Marilyn Peretti
Glen Ellyn, IL

Being a Chicagoan
in honor of Laquan McDonald
and all the others

Am I a Chicagoan? Not really.
I live way out here, but aren't
we all Chicagoans? Aren't we
all the young men seeking
jobs on the police force,
aren't we all the Mayor
looking the other way,
aren't we all the well-off
and the lesser and the
least wishing for more?

Then why? Why do we
continue to close doors,
practice segregation
and 21st century
lynching? Lynching?
Hanging in a tree? No,
just no tree, forget
the tree: just kill
because he's black:
just rid of him since
he is not understood,
he is simply walking,
he is testing you,

since you have nothing
better to do, you have
a gun, you have orders,
you have power, you
have the bullets, you
have the ugly heart,
you have the ignorance.

Your face blazes
with ignorance.

Iris Orpi
Chicago, IL

16 Silences

To echo as the light had echoed
on the hour when it was all
that was left in the house
that was home to stuffy silences
and stray bullets
of dreams

to feel what the hush must have felt
when it fell
in the narrow gaps between gunshots
brushing past the last words
snatched from his lips
and the certainty that he was dead

to speak his name
a year too late
and be the anger drawn like cursed lots
on the lottery of living
and being kept in the dark
like dirty, lie stained secrets

to believe what the city believes
when it takes up the fight
another day

to bleed on the edges of the torn open
blindness, and replace
one handicap for another
and not be afraid
to ask for change
like children
who look at the leafless trees
and ask questions about the future
as if the connection were
as natural to them as
opening their eyes after
a night of sleep

David Nekimken

Chicago, IL

The Value of Life in Death

The images stream in an endless loop
Explosions interrupting a soccer match
Military flooding Parisian streets
Newscasters repeating "breaking news"
Every ten or fifteen minutes
Analysts and experts speculating
Pontificating about Paris vulnerability
Regional terrorists gone global
Horrific, unprecedented, evil acts.

An American drone destroys a hospital
In faraway Afghanistan
41 patients and medical staff dead
Sorry, an unfortunate accident
Promised investigation
Soon disappearing from media memory.

A black youth killed by a policeman
Local story goes national
Perhaps global
Community tensions and outrage
Expressions of grief
Calls for forgiveness
Calls to examine our national culture
Violence and guns
Militarization of police
Unsupported troubled youth.

Are some killings more horrific than others?
Are some lives more sacred than others?
Do the details of a killing make some killings more reprehensible?

Mary Jo Balistreri
Waukesha, WI

flow, n

1.plentiful; a copious supply; extravagantly demonstrative; *ordinary norms did not apply to him.* 2. gradual and permanent deformation of a solid under stress; *he shop-lifted comics* and *cars as a child.* 3. tide of passion; *obsessed with a girl he could not have.* 4. to rise and fall like a flood; work; *he rose to the top, fell to the bottom, drifted and stalked.* 5. as in an electric current; *veins filled with adrenaline, he took a gun from his brother's cabinet.* 6. wine poured out unstintingly; *his bottle— empty.* 7. data flowing between computers simultaneously; glints of light; the unconscious running undisturbed; *trigger happy boy, a ladder to a girl's bedroom, flashes of light, black out*

Jennifer May
St. Charles, IL

Your Unnaming

Child within -
making me Mother
I nourished myself --
nourished you.
More than one
was somehow two.
I dreamed your name
girl child. Pink.
I bore you. I carried you.
Then growing up yearly

but with growing dimness in your eyes
you receded to hard shell.
Clashing, fiercely crashing
and anchor heavy
your eyes grew dimmer still.
Going under your black oceans
with swallowed salty word water drowning
You sought only death
and my heart
contracted.

We are one but two.
Cyanotic
purpling.
My palms to your chest.
Push, rest, push, rest—
pinch nose—
blow.

You learned the word.
Transcribed.

A breath.
Translated.

Transgender.

Blue.
You; boy child.
Shining.
I unname you.

Name yourself.

John Gordon
La Grange, IL

Eulogies Needed

for tear-choked memorial services
and funerals of gun victims

The killers are triggered by
fear rage mental illness drugs
revenge greed a cause self defense...
but also by accident and irreversible mistake

Flesh-ripping bullets erupt from an array
of cheap mass-produced to exquisite hand-crafted
pistols rifles shotguns and assault weapons
with uniformly fatal results

This non-stop carnage performs
a modern *dance of death*
choreographed by corporate greed
partnered with inflamed paranoia
directed by constitutional ignorance

Personal freedom alone can never justify
the bizarre proposals put forth
to reduce rampant gun violence

Provide more guns   (300 million plus are insufficient)

Prepare more eulogies

Robin Lily Goldberg

River Forest, IL

nomadic mazes

Where can we go
        when time turns inside out
    within our skin?

        when pillows fail
    to provide canopies
        for our dreams?

        when tears
    become too tangible
            to convey empathy?

Tracie Renee Amirante Padal

Palatine, IL

March

Above a path where fisted fingers
shattered glass,

       one red bird waits
    on a burnt stub of branch:
             singing.

6.
Protest Days

Judith MK Kaufman
Highland Park, IL

Heart Burn

Years ago
I swallowed a sponge
which traveled
past my teeth and tongue
over my gullet and likely
down my windpipe
absorbing on its way
any bits of bile
it might encounter
sucking out any
possibility of explosion.

The sponge has now
completed its route,
exited my body and,
in its wake, allowed
a fire to spread
along its former route
ashes lodging in my throat
to irritate, exacerbate
ultimately detonate
expelling past
my teeth and tongue
blasting words
I never knew
were in me.

Gerda Govine Ituarte
Pasadena, CA

Long Haul

Protest

Again   Risk

Over   Afraid

All   Stay

Start   Slip on

Up   High wire

Get   Tumble

Down

Chicago, IL

Gloved Protest for Love

Pink green red purple black
On gold
Pair over pair oh pair
Hushed tolled
Whispery soft

Dusty earth yawns open, track
T'is told.
Voice upon voice, O Voice!
Weak, bold,
Misery loft.

Beverly M. Collins
Burbank, CA

Waves

So threatened by growth are the
tiny-intended. So alarmed are the
note-less by a song.

Oppressors can slink like a
doe-eyed serpent; An assailant
that seeks to wound with teeth
concealed.

Oppressors- trapped in need to feel
superior while seated upon another,

covet foolhearted desires as fruitless
as a dream to punch sunlight from the sky
to ban its beams from a landscape.

Oppressors press voices into a massive
heat of one collective call for freedom.

They press the perceived weaker party,
into greater muscle, into stronger associations,
into waves of larger alignment that
can (and will) overcome.

Michael P Wright

Highwood, IL

Protest Days

Anarchy, revolt, protest, a first amendment blessing
Classically American, the right to protest, a precious thought
Such cringing proletariat, is pondering and wondering
The sovereignty of thought reigns supreme

Argue your sentiments, the battleground is all set
The outspoken few are embarking on their right to self-righteous protest
A mission for revolutionary change
Fraught with articulation and clear motives

Bantering, posturing, screaming, quite the faux accompli
Their ends justify their means
Brilliance bestowed or will the government seize their brilliant protocols
Protests make the world evolve

Mom's family would join the protesters for apple pie
Protesting as the American way necessary to illicit subversive trends
Internal protests an everyday occurrence
A quixotic analysis and dissection of what protests really means.

Peter Rodenby
United Kingdom

They told us in the sixty's
[or the lament of an old English Socialist]

They told us in the sixty's
we would all retire young
Men and women,
fifty five was spoken of in those days.
When we were naive we believed them
our country would take care of us
from cradle to grave.
We took that for granted
 it was the socialist way.
It was right and true.
They told us in the seventy's
 computers would do the work
give us more free time.
Our future looked so rosy.
A three day week was on the cards
 A Thirty hour working week
and all the rest a holiday
It was too good to be true
but that's what they said.
I remember.
They tell us now
 we all must work much longer
at more than one poor paid job
And be grateful for employment.
"Retirement is for wasters, work is good for you"

The IT Revolution has robbed workers
Of work and skill and not content with that
I now must have a private pension fund
Medical insurance and a funeral policy.
"You can't expect your country to pay for you in old age".
I have worked my turn I want my fun
It's my time to travel, play and run.
A happy retirement without fear
Still alive and healthy one of the few
"They "have betrayed us
as they betrayed. our fathers.
Capitalism keeps changing
Like the face of evil
But workers are still martyrs to the system

Deborah Stoker

United Kingdom

'Job's not me'

Verse 1:
As the dark mornings beckon and the clock hands are in place,
It's time to an-ti-ci-pate the day's tasks, now you're in the rat-race.
That warm but oh so moist pillow, evidence of a stormy night,
Those unsightly psychological images, remind me things just aren't quite right.
Fibres underfoot, every step reluctantly taken,
Hair brush bristles tear across my cranium, stone floor felt, spirits awaken,
Laboriously long hours and com-plete-ly misguided,
Corporate natures, monotony, I have indeed become affected.

Chorus:
Job's just not me, can't you see, uniform behaviour is frowning back at me,
So own up, act right now, step right back and take a bow,
I've had my share, got nothing else to spare, it's just not me, me, me,
Looking at pastures new, new, new.

Verse 2:
I reached for the water, calm, pure and still,
Enveloped by clammy, shaking skin-careful not to spill,
Barely visible, through salt swollen vision,
To cope-breathe-exist, too aware of the mission.
Trapped in a corner, ensnared by life's game,
A million and one chores, balance books, won't stay the same.

Chorus:
Job's just not me, can't you see, uniform behaviour is frowning back at me,
So own up, act right now, step right back and take a bow,
I've had my share, got nothing else to spare, it's just not me, me, me,
Looking at pastures new, new, new.

Verse 3:
Curtains opened rigorously, say goodbye to my photo of Michael,
Acknowledge the sodden weeping willow tree, prepared for its next cycle,
Fortress locked for the day, prosperity and growth at the forefront,
The grips of repetitive, robotic occurrences, there's definitely cause for a shunt.
Time to leave checked back and front, collar up and iPod's in,
Done selflessly, unwillingly for brethren and kin,
Yeah, yeah, oh yeah, for brethren and kin.

Chorus:
Job's just not me, can't you see, uniform behaviour is frowning back at me,
So own up, act right now, step right back and take a bow,
I've had my share, got nothing else to spare, it's just not me, me, me,
Looking at pastures new, new, new.

Verse 4:
Try, try, try, you'll eventually succeed,
Efforts will be rewarded, evolved from a different breed,
Living in the here and now, atrophy creeps in only when paused,
Only one more month to go, it's written as a clause.

Chorus:
Job's just not me, can't you see, uniform behaviour is frowning back at me,
So own up, act right now, step right back and take a bow,
I've had my share, got nothing else to spare, it's just not me, me, me,
Looking at pastures new, new, new.

Joseph Schlesinger
Chicago, IL

Surrender, My Captor

Dark days elapse; it's come to this,
Then: ages pass, leading to . . . what?
Alone and lost, yet I've waited
To learn why you've betrayed my trust.
I don't know what you want from me.
Still, I'm bound to you each moment.

Your spell unbroken, this moment
Crushes my soul--and all for this?
I don't know what you want from me.
Is it innocence? Tell me what.
I yearn for someone I can trust,
But in vain, it seems, I've waited.

Long I've languished, wondered, waited
From moment to anguished moment,
With no rescue in sight. I trust
My strength will stand through all of this--
And still no clue to what is what.
I don't know what you want from me.

I don't know what you want from me.
I steel myself, but you've waited
Patiently for me to give what
I can never give. The moment
I accede will nullify this
Remnant of faith in which I trust.

It becomes a matter of trust.
I don't know what you want from me.
I wish I didn't care, but this
Trust might mean my freedom: I've waited
For an answer, sought the moment
When I can conquer you. So what?

For you to have your way is what
Would destroy me, so I must trust
In my endurance. That moment
When I know what you want from me
Will never come. Having waited
To lay my plans, I pray for this . . .

   I don't know what you want from me.
   Carte blanche? Blind trust? I have waited
   For this moment, too. Here, take this.

Ken Brown

Evanston, IL

The American Dream: Welcome to the Bear

I feel like I'm drifting away. That stormy sea of life. In rough waters.
I want to find shelter. Away. Not be involved. I don't feel connected.
I don't have the same ambition as the programmed. Conditioned.
Bred of consumership culture in greed of tyrants and hierarchy that exist indeed.

Similar to a dream. Another dimension.
For they are not in the very same waters that are stormy.
They splash. Sit in comfort. Safe on land. Sturdy.
Let the others do it. As they capitalize. Manipulate.

Entwining the American Dream to that illusion. To Be Somebody.
Yet, content in a white picket fence.
Follow. Be in order. You will be fulfilling your purpose.
What you don't know is, it's already been decided for you, by the elite.
The Ones above. Keeping a blanket over our eyes. Implementing.

Starting from childhood in our education system. Into that climbing the ladder.
That continuous chase. Fitting grooves, aligning your place.
Buy into the tricks of grandeur and illusions to be consumers.
On hamster wheels sprinting. Going nowhere.
But continuously believe that running is going somewhere.

It was conditioning of the thinking. Walking straight, with blinders on.
Only seeing what you're allowed. If you look to the side, you may question your direction.
THEY DON'T WANT THAT. They like watching us squirm. Fighting. Battling.
Like salmon swimming upstream. Thrusting mightily. Only to find themselves in jaws.

WELCOME TO THE BEAR.

It was all false. Not real. It was a façade. They almost fooled me. I believed.
But I no longer choose to swim upstream. I will look to the sides. Know my direction.
Lift off the blanket. See reality. Free from outer forces.
My power within will rectify throughout.
They will know. They will see. Upon my reckoning!

Nancy Lind
Pasadena, CA

Bang

In these restless winter years,
Kids, this is where Grandma
Chooses a thrill that may be an exit.
(I wish you'd all close your jaws.)

I adored Amelia Earhart,
As a girl. She took risks.
Her poetic adventures,
Piloting a plane that looked like tinfoil,
Became a lasting myth.

        Now, for my thrill,
Something must move me, literally —
A wing suit so that I could fly
Like a bat, off El Capitan at dawn,
Kite-surfing, hang-gliding, ballooning,
Sky diving --
(Yes, I've actually charted such excitements.)

       I've got it!
Tropical parasailing, holding tight
To my gaudy parachute as the speed boat
Blasts off, eye-to-eye with passing pelicans,
Staring at me as a strange new creature
In their sky, while I gaze down, astonished,
To the ocean far below, dazzling with fish
Of every shape, size, color, stripes, spots --
As if seeing a world with the eye of God,
Wondrous, all beauty, and right.

It'll be enough.

ABOUT THE PROTESTERS

Beverly M. Collins is the author of the books *Quiet Observations: Diary Thought, Whimsy and Rhyme* and *Mud in Magic*. She was a winner in the California State Poetry Society competition and has been nominated for the Pushcart Prize and Best Independent American Poetry for her work in *Rubicon: Words & Art Inspired by Oscar Wilde's De Profundis*. She was born in Delaware and grew up in New Jersey.

Casey Derengowski honed his writing skills as a probation officer and, in retirement, is an active member of the Lake San Marcos Writers' Group.

CJ Laity is the publisher and editor of Chicago Poetry Press through which he has published over twenty anthologies of poetry. He is the author of several poetry books as well as three published fiction titles. He has been active as a poetry promoter in Chicago for thirty years.

David Nekimken is a senior citizen living in Qumbya Housing Cooperative in Hyde Park, Chicago. He is a graduate of Antioch College in Ohio and a former member of the Neighborhood Writers Alliance.

Deborah Nodler Rosen is the author of several books including *sight/seer*, a collection of her travel poems, and *ANWAR EL SADAT*, a biography of the Egyptian leader. In addition she has edited the book *Where We Find Ourselves: Jewish Women Around the World Write about Home*. Rosen is an editor of *RHINO*, an award-winning poetry journal, and teaches poetry workshops in the school.

Deborah Stoker lives in Newcastle upon Tyne, North East England. She studied English Literature at Northumbria University where she graduated with honors. She has two wonderful children.

Diane O'Neill has had work published in *South Side Weekly* and upcoming in *The Shine Journal*. Her essays have been published in *The Chicago Tribune* and National University's *Gnu Journal*. She is an active member of the KIDSCRIT critique group and MISSING VOICE, a Facebook discussion group promoting diverse picture books.

Donal Mahoney, a native of Chicago, lives in St. Louis, Missouri. He has worked as an editor for *The Chicago Sun-Times*, Loyola University Press in Chicago and at Washington University in St. Louis. He has had fiction and poetry published in *The Wisconsin Review, The Kansas Quarterly, The South Carolina Review, The Christian Science Monitor, The Beloit Poetry Journal, Commonweal, The Galway Review* (Ireland), *The Osprey Journal* (Wales), *Public Republic* (Bulgaria), and *The Istanbul Literary Review* (Turkey).

Gerda Govine Ituarte has been writing most of her life as a teacher, college administrator, journalist, researcher and grant writer. She is the author of the books *Oh, Where is My Candle Hat?* (2012) and *Alterations | Thread Light Through Eye of Storm* (2015), and her work has appeared in such journals as *Dryland L.A. Arts and Letters, Coiled Serpent, Altadena Poetry Review, San Gabriel Valley Poetry Review,* and *Spectrum Magazine*. She has had the opportunity to read her work in Canada, Colombia, Cuba, U.K. and Mexico.

Iris Orpi is a Filipina writer living in Lansing, Illinois. She is the author of the novel *The Espresso Effect* (2010) and two books of compiled poems *Beautiful Fever* (2012) and *Cognac for the Soul* (2012). Her poems and essays have appeared in over a dozen publications in Asia, the United States and the United Kingdom.

Itala Langmar is an Illinois artist and has been painting and writing poetry since she was a girl in Venice, Italy. After gaining proficiency in English, she began writing poetry in English as well as Italian. Itala often informs her paintings with the text of her poems because choosing the right words and the perfect colors for them are mutually creative.

Jeff Rogers dropped out of college in 1983 and drove a rust-fringed Chevy Malibu to Los Angeles, where he has lived ever since. He has had two poems published in *The Coiled Serpent* published by Luis J. Rodriguez, Poet Laureate of Los Angeles. His work has also appeared in *The Altar Collective, Volume VIII, The Altadena Review Anthology 2016, Spectrum* and is a featured poet for the online journal *Archive 405*. His poem "Give Me Questions" first appeared at Avenue50Studio.org

Jennifer Dotson is the founder and program coordinator for HighlandParkPoetry.org. Her poems have been published in *East On Central, After Hours, Poetry Cram* and *A Midnight Snack* from Poetic License Press. She teaches creative writing and memoir for District 113's Continuing Education Program. Jennifer Dotston is the first recipient of the JOMP Book Award for her manuscript Clever Gretel.

Jennifer May is a co-founder of Open Sky Poets in the Fox Valley area, a group dedicated to literary education and critique. She was recently published in the *Kane County Chronicle Poets Corner*. She was a two-year editor for the fine arts magazines *Towers and Byzantium*. Her poem "Winter Trees" earned special recognition at the Danada Fine Arts Festival.

Jim Davis is a student of Human Development and Psychology at Harvard University and has previously studied at Northwestern University and Knox College. He reads for TriQuarterly and his work has appeared in *Bellevue Literary Review, Harpur Palate, The Harvard Crimson, Portland Review, RHINO, Midwest Quarterly,* and *California Journal of Poetics*, among others. He has received multiple Pushcart Prize and Best of the Net nominations and won many contests, including the Line Zero Poetry Prize. In addition to writing and painting, Jim is an international semi-professional American football player.

Joan Krieger Hoffman is a poet living in North Hollywood, California.

John J. Gordon is married and has three children and eight grandchildren. He is a member and former officer of the Illinois State Poetry Society and Poets & Patrons and has been published in *JOMP 15, 16*, and *17* as well as in *Prairie Light Review, Beaver Island Reader* and on several internet sites.

Joseph ("Joe") Glaser spent most of his career in technology, but, in retirement, he pursued Liberal Arts and began writing poetry in 2008. His poems have appeared in print in *The Journal* (Northwestern University OLLI program), *Journal of Modern Poetry* through which he won the JOMP 16 Best Modern Poem Prize, and in *Distilled Lives Vol 2* (Illinois State Poetry Society). Joe also pursues candid travel photography and his photos have been published in the same media as his poetry.

Joseph Schlesinger lives in Chicago with his sansevieria. His work has appeared in *Texas Quarterly* and *Journal of Modern Poetry*.

Judith MK Kaufman is the Editor-in-Chief of *East on Central*, a Journal of Literature and Art from Highland Park, Illinois, which has recently published its fourteenth annual edition. Judith's work has been published in *Poetica, Collage, Poetry Cram 9, Journal of Modern Poetry 16* and online at *Pirene's Fountain* and *Highland Park Poetry*.

Kathy Lundy Derengowski is a Southern California poet active in the poetry community of North San Diego County. She has been a finalist in the San Diego Book Awards poetry chapbook category, and is currently co-submissions editor for *Summation*, the anthology from the poets and artists of the Escondido Municipal Gallery.

Ken Brown, aka, Christopher Leadway is an actor/writer/performer who has spent the last couple years writing and developing a persona with "a dark perspective, distorted reality with abstract illustrations that is borderline insanity." He plans to introduce this in live sets, utilizing multi-media performed at open poetry readings and slams.

Linda Leedy Schneider, winner in the 2012 Contemporary American Poetry Prize, is a political activist, poetry and writing mentor and psychotherapist in private practice. She founded The Manhattan Writing Workshop and conducts workshops for The International Women's Writing Guild. Linda has written six collections of poetry and edited two collections written by poets whom she has mentored.

Margaret Dubay Mikus, Ph.D. was a research scientist who healed from multiple sclerosis and cancer. Now a poet, singer and photographer, she is the author of three books of poetry. In 2013 she was the Illinois Featured Author for the *Willow Review*.

Marian Kaplun Shapiro was nominated for the Pushcart Prize in 2012. A Quaker and a psychologist specializing in the results of trauma, she is an unabashed peacenik. A five-time Senior Poet Laureate of Massachusetts, she is the author of a professional book and many related articles, one full-length poetry book and two chapbooks.

Marilyn Peretti writes with poet colleagues in the western suburbs of Chicago. She has published the books *Let Wings Take You, To Remember-To Hope, Lichen-Poems of Nature,* and *Angel's Wings.* She has been published in *Talking River, Fox Cry Review, Christian Science Monitor, Journal of Modern Poetry, California Quarterly, www.poetrysky.com, Kyoto Journal* and others. Visit pagesbyperetti.com and perettipoems.wordpress.com.

Mary Jo Balistreri has published two books of poetry through Bellowing Ark Press and a chapbook through Tiger's Eye Press. She enjoys reading, long walks and gardening. Visit her at maryjobalistreripoet.com.

Mary Langer Thompson's poetry appears in various journals and anthologies. She is a contributor to *The Working Poet* (Autumn Press) and *Women and Poetry: Tips on Writing, Teaching and Publishing by Successful Women Poets* (McFarland). She is a former school principal with an Ed.D. from the University of California, Los Angeles.

Michael P Wright is a poet residing in Highwood, Illinois, a small community sandwiched between Ft Sheridan, Lake Forest and Highland Park. Michael says: "The thought of writing is exhilarating." He enjoys attending workshops and poetry readings throughout the North Shore.

Nancy J. Heggem is a retired mathematician and former Trustee of the Palatine Public Library District. She is active with Northwest Cultural Council Poets and sponsors the annual poetry contest at the Palatine Public Library. Her work has been published in a number of Chicago area anthologies.

Nancy Lind is a retired professor of English literature and a lifetime Dickensian. She has studied poetry in workshops with award winning poets Dan Masterson and Mira Mataric. Nancy has been a member and sometimes founder of several literary groups. She currently resides in Pasadena, CA and has been active in regional poetry events. Most recently Nancy's poems have been published in *Impulse* and the *Altadena Poetry Review.*

Pamela Borovich is a freelance writer and poet currently attending Nursing School full time. She has authored and illustrated the children's book *Sandy the Sharing Seagull* which was awarded a coveted spot on the 2010 KART Book List by the South Jersey Children's Literary Festival. She has been featured in *Poetry Cram 10 and 12* and *Journal of Modern Poetry 15.*

Peter Rodenby is a retired electrical engineer and full time grandfather who lives in an old cottage by a river with his wife. He has a degree in Earth Science and enjoys studying history and literature.

Robin Lily Goldberg published her first poem at age six in *Spider Magazine*. After studying creative writing at Kenyon College and the University of Michigan, she published her first book of poetry, *Sound of Seeds*. When not writing, she teaches yoga and contributes to a storytelling program for hospital patients.

S. M. Kozubek is an attorney, author and teacher. He has been published in *ICON, Frogpond, A Hundred Gourds, Prune Juice* and *bottle rockets*.

Tamara Tabel received a Silver Prize from Chicago Poetry Press for her poem "Albeit Macht Frei: Dachau 2012" which was subsequently selected to be included in *Poetica Magazine's* 2014 Holocaust Edition.

Thelma T. Reyna is a multiple national award-winning author and a Poet Laureate in Southern California. Her full-length collection of poetry *Rising, Falling, All of Us* has received national honors.

Tobin Fraley is the author of three books on the history of carousels, one children's book as well as the book *36 Acres*, a photographic and written exploration of the Reed-Turner Woodland Nature Preserve in Long Grove, Illinois. He is founder and director of the not-for-profit Long Grove Arts & Music Council (lgamc.org), member of the Barrington Writers Workshop, photography teacher at Chicago Botanic Gardens and a product designer.

Tracie Renee Amirante Padal's short stories and poems have won contests sponsored by *Scholastic, Seventeen, USA Weekend*, Xerox/DocuWorld, the Northwest Cultural Council, and Highland Park Poetry, and she has been published in *The Daily Herald, Bark, In Our Own Words: a Generation Defining Itself* and in the literary journals A*pocalypse, The Claremont Review, Louisville Review, Moon Journal*, and *Oyez Review.*

Tricia Marcella Cimera has been published in *Buddhist Poetry Review, Foliate Oak, Hedgerow, Mad Swirl, Silver Birch Press*, and *Yellow Chair Review*. Her poem "The Swear Poem" was first published online at *I Am Not A Silent Poet*, November 2015.

Trudy Leong earned an Associate in the Arts in May 2015 at Wilbur Wright College where she served as Editor-in-Chief of The Wright Side and coordinated twelve poetry slams. She now pursues a bachelor's in business administration at Northeastern Illinois University.

Wilda Morris has been very busy in the poetry world over the past several years as Workshop Chair of Poets & Patrons, Secretary of the Illinois State Poetry Society, and Email Director of the Rockford Writers' Guild. She has also served as Chair of the Stevens Poetry Manuscript Competition of the National Federation of State Poetry Societies. She recently attended writers' workshops in Orvieto, Italy and in Mexico.

CHICAGO POETRY PRESS

Made in the USA
Charleston, SC
16 April 2016